W9-AWE-152

SECRET SERVICE

© Aladdin Books Ltd 1988

Designed and produced by
Aladdin Books Ltd
70 Old Compton Street
London W1

Design: Rob Hillier
Editor: Catherine Bradley
Researcher: Cecilia Weston-Baker
Illustrator: Ron Hayward Associates

First published in the
United States in 1988 by
Gloucester Press
387 Park Avenue South
New York, NY 10016

Library of Congress Catalog
Card Number: 87-82888

Printed in Belgium

ISBN 0-531-17079-9

The front cover shows a Soviet agent meeting a German contact in a wood near Cologne in West Germany, 1966.
The back cover shows a Lockheed SR-71 spy plane, the most expensive camera in the world.

The author, Duncan Campbell, is a staff writer and investigative reporter for the New Statesman magazine, London.

The consultant, Dr. John Pimlott, is a Senior Lecturer in the Department of War Studies at the Royal Military Academy, Sandhurst, U.K. He is an expert on international relations and security matters.

Contents

SECRET SERVICE

DUNCAN CAMPBELL

Illustrated by
Ron Hayward Associates

GLOUCESTER PRESS
New York : London : Toronto : Sydney

Introduction

Some of the world's bestselling books are about spies or secret agents. Real secret service activity is not as exciting as that created by spy novelists. But new developments or crises in the spy business occur daily. Most countries have at least one secret service, which spies on its own people as well as on other nations.

When secret services gather information about new political, military or economic developments, it is called "intelligence." Secret services often have official titles such as "intelligence agency." The most famous secret services are the Soviet KGB (*Komitet Gosudarstvennoy Bezopasnosti* – Committee for State Security), the American Central Intelligence Agency (CIA), and the British Secret Intelligence Service (known as MI6).

By providing advance warning of unexpected political or military developments, secret services can change the course of history. Most countries are less willing to admit that they operate secret services in peacetime, than during war. Since the end of the Second World War, intelligence agencies worldwide have flourished, building up power and commanding enormous budgets. It is thought that the US agencies' annual expenditure is $7,500,000,000. But is this money well spent?

◁ West and East Germany exchange spies, Alice Michelsen and Wolfgang Vogel, in June 1985. In 1945 Germany was divided into two. Many people have family ties and loyalties to both countries, which secret agents on both sides can use to recruit spies.

Why have spies?

▽ Peter Wright was a British intelligence officer. In 1986, he became famous after the British government tried to ban his book of memoirs, *Spycatcher*. He claimed that the former head of an intelligence agency (MI5), Roger Hollis, had been a Soviet spy. He also revealed that MI5 officers had been involved in plans to overthrow the British Labor government in the 1960s.

Spying means obtaining information that other countries do not want revealed. Sometimes this information can be as vital as news of a planned invasion or war. But whether countries are at war or at peace, international espionage battles conducted by human spies and space age surveillance systems go on every day.

Spying is one of the ways that secret services use to get information. Much information is openly gathered by journalists and news agencies. Diplomats and ambassadors posted to a foreign country are legally and officially expected and allowed to collect information and send it back. Such information is a major part of the intelligence business.

Because it is legally obtained, it is said to come from open sources. The other method for collecting information is from covert (hidden) sources. They are hidden because such methods are usually illegal.

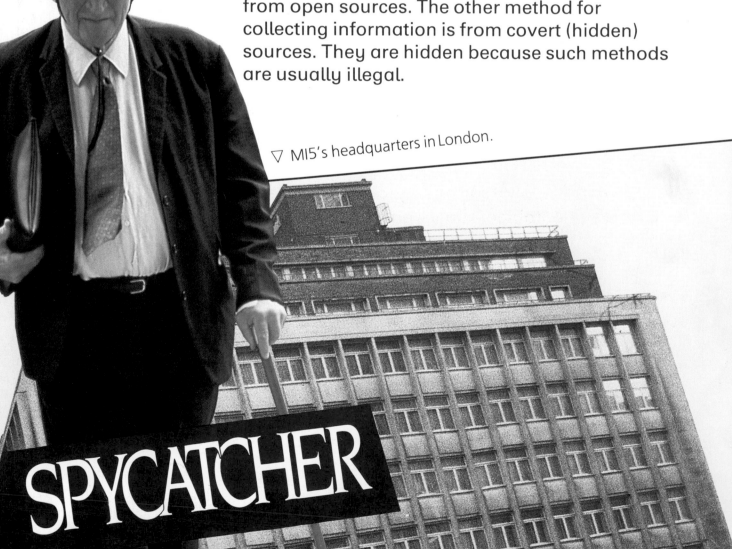

▽ MI5's headquarters in London.

SPYCATCHER

Another government's biggest secrets cannot usually be obtained from open sources, since the government will try to make sure that such information is never published. This kind of secret information usually includes military and defense plans – and information about the country's own secret services. Espionage or using spies is one way to obtain such material.

But many spy writers argue that the amount of information collected by covert means is small compared to the information which can be collected openly. The claims by the secret services about their importance are often greatly exaggerated.

△ The Soviet ambassador, Anatoly Dobrynin, returns to Moscow in 1986 after 24 years in the United States. Having spent so long abroad, Dobrynin had excellent relations with many top US officials. In fact, in 1978 the KGB suspected him of spying for the United States. He was cleared. Diplomats enjoy some protection from the law and are in a better position to obtain information from official sources than other foreigners.

Secret operations

In 1987, the Iran-*Contra* affair in the United States reminded the world that spying on other countries is not all that secret services do. The most controversial activities of a secret service are often its covert operations. This means that the secret service does not just try to spy on and gather information about another country. Instead, it tries to interfere directly in the other country's affairs.

Examples of covert operations have included plans to assassinate foreign leaders, such as Fidel Castro of Cuba, or attempts to overthrow a foreign government and replace it with a more sympathetic one. In 1984 it was discovered that the CIA had been assisting the anti-government *Contras* in Nicaragua by supervising the mining of Nicaraguan harbors. Because Congress was not informed of this action, it forbade any US military aid to the *Contras*.

△ TOW anti-tank missiles (top) were sold to the Iranians in the arms-for-hostages scandal. Colonel Oliver North (above) was involved in this covert operation, which led to the sending of funds to the Nicaraguan *Contras*.

8

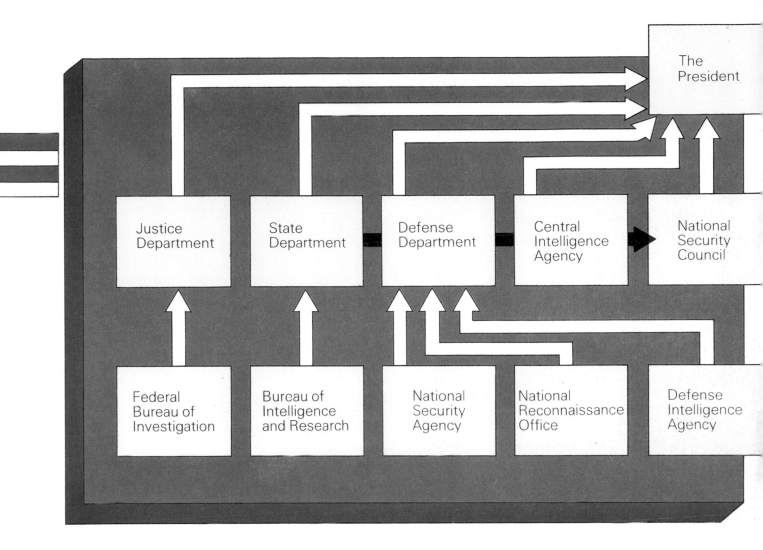

In the Iran-*Contra* affair, the American government secretly sold military equipment to Iran. Officially the government had declared that it would not deal with Iran because it was a terrorist state. The secret arms trade was supposed to secure the freedom of several US hostages held in Lebanon. This never happened. The equipment was sold at a profit, and the profits were then used to pay for arms for the *Contras*. This was illegal.

The operation was conducted by an officer in the National Security Council (NSC), Oliver North. He claimed that President Ronald Reagan was informed about the operation. But his superior, the NSC adviser to the President, then testified that this was not the case. If the President did not know about these secret dealings, then the US government is no longer in control of its secret agencies.

△ The United States has the largest secret service in the West. Apart from the well-known CIA, the Federal Bureau of Investigation (FBI) is responsible for internal security and catching spies; the National Security Agency (NSA) is a gigantic international electronic monitoring organization; the National Reconnaissance Office (NRO) operates spy satellites; and the Defense Intelligence Agency (DIA) gathers intelligence for US military forces. The official US Secret Service is a security organization for the President and other important public officials for whom it provides bodyguards.

Western secret services

Most countries in the world now have their own secret services. However the power of these bodies depends on how much money they get.

Although spies and secret agents are older than the Bible, permanently established secret services are a 20th century development. The British Secret Intelligence Service, MI6, was set up in 1909, together with a counterespionage department to detect spies, called MI5. Britain now spends about $1.65 billion every year on these security and intelligence agencies. About half of this money is spent on the British electronic monitoring agency, called GCHQ. GCHQ cooperates with the American NSA and smaller agencies in Australia, Canada and New Zealand. Although not as closely linked as the English-speaking secret services, members of the North Atlantic Treaty Organization (NATO) also exchange the intelligence they gather.

▽ Greenpeace is an international environmental protection group. In July 1985, two agents of the French secret service (below) planted mines on the Greenpeace yacht, *Rainbow Warrior*. One man was killed and the boat was sunk. The purpose of this official French government terrorist action was to prevent the yacht from disrupting French nuclear tests in the south Pacific Ocean.

All these countries have agreed to collaborate in their spying efforts so that secret agencies do not try to spy on the same thing. Their cooperation includes directing human spies as well as electronic listening stations and spy satellites. The 1980s have seen a dramatic expansion of surveillance of all types of communications. This makes it increasingly difficult to analyze the large amount of material collected. During the 1982 Falklands (Malvinas) War, British intelligence agencies failed to predict the Argentinian invasion of the islands – despite receiving material indicating this was likely.

Western secret services, like their Eastern counterparts, have used terrorist tactics and sabotage for political purposes. At other times, they collaborate to detect and prevent terrorism – particularly international terrorism coming from Middle Eastern countries.

▽ In August 1987 Margaret Hoeke was found guilty of spying and sentenced to eight years' imprisonment. She is one of many West German secretaries who have been uncovered by counter-espionage agents. It was discovered that she had been betraying secrets out of love. Her boyfriend had asked her to pass on documents from her office, where she worked for the West German President.

△ Following various spy scandals, the West German government produced a poster warning secretaries not to befriend strangers in cafes because they might be agents trying to trick them.

Eastern spies

The KGB is thought to be the world's largest secret service organization. With the assistance of the Soviet military intelligence organization, GRU, it is responsible for espionage and counterespionage, as well as internal security and guarding Soviet borders and nuclear weapons installations.

The intelligence agencies of other Warsaw Pact countries such as Poland, Hungary or Czechoslovakia are usually thought to work under the overall direction of the KGB.

Spies working for the KGB, as for other secret services, often pretend to be diplomats. In major cities such as Washington, New York, London and Paris, as many as 200 so-called Soviet diplomats may be spies, working undercover. When they are detected, they are often expelled, sometimes in large numbers.

According to Western intelligence experts, the KGB's main activity in the 1980s was to obtain technology secrets from the West. Much of this information was obtained openly from newspapers and trade journals. High technology equipment was also bought on the open market by the Soviet Union.

△ In September 1985 more than 40 Soviet diplomats and journalists were expelled from Great Britain. The British government, acting on information from the security services, claimed that all the diplomats were spies. It is unlikely that many of the people expelled in such a large group were actually caught spying. But counterespionage services can guess who are the real diplomats and who are not, from their patterns of activity, which are now regularly watched. In Moscow, KGB officials keep a close watch on Western diplomats for the same reason.

▷ Colonel Vladimir Izmaylov was an air attache at the Soviet embassy in Washington, D.C. He was arrested in June 1986 when he tried to collect secret documents bought from a US Air Force officer, who was working with the Federal Bureau of Investigation. He was immediately ordered to leave.

▽ The former KGB headquarters, Lubyanka, in Moscow used to be offices. It was converted to include a prison and was known as "the Center." The KGB's task is to preserve the Communist Party's power. In fact, in 1982 the KGB chief Yuri Andropov became the Communist Party leader.

What is intelligence?

The information collected by secret services can include material about a country's political activity, business, industry, farming, transportation, power supplies and other factors which affect relations with other countries. Secret services also need to find out about other countries' armed forces and military potential and preparedness.

Most people working for intelligence services work in an ordinary office and for the same hours as any other office worker. Much of their time is spent analyzing the information collected by their service, its agents and other surveillance systems, and turning it into reports for other parts of the government.

Just like a private business, the secret service has to ask its customers (such as government ministers and military leaders) to say what intelligence they most want. Then the secret service decides how it will try to get that information, and how great an effort it will make to get it.

▽ Soviet leaders at a parade of military hardware held every year in November to celebrate the Russian Revolution. Military equipment and plans are usually the highest priority intelligence gathering work for a secret service. But political information is even more important. It is very useful for Western governments to know what the Soviet leaders are thinking and planning. In the 1970s a Soviet official in the Global Affairs Department gave the United States hundreds of documents outlining foreign policy plans. After the KGB arrested him, he committed suicide.

It could plan to use spies, to ask diplomats to make open inquiries, or just start reading the right newspapers. After the intelligence has been collected it is analyzed and put together, to see if information from different sources matches up, and to see what data is still missing. Then the intelligence analyst has to tell the government what the conclusions are.

It is very important that intelligence analysis is honest and that secret services do not try to tell governments what they think they want to hear. For example, it is likely that before the Soviet invasion of Afghanistan in 1979, the KGB did not assess the possibility of Afghan resistance correctly.

The process of gathering intelligence is repeated continuously. Secret services try to follow up new developments, or improve their estimates of what is happening in a particular target country. But sometimes rivalry between different agencies within a country means not all the information is put together.

▷ The MX missile is the latest United States long-range intercontinental nuclear ballistic missile. For more than 10 years, US strategists have worked on plans to hide such missiles from the enemy. Plans have included launching the missiles from mobile railroad trucks or road transporters.

Secret listeners

Telephone tapping and bugging are some of the best known technical methods which secret services use to help gather information. When a telephone is tapped, extra cables are attached to the target telephone line. These cables go to a listening post, where telephone calls from the target telephone can be monitored. Usually, a tape recorder is connected to the line. It automatically starts recording as soon as the telephone is picked up. The new equipment is so sophisticated it is difficult to detect.

But ordinary conversation in a room cannot be monitored by a telephone tap when the telephone is not being used. Instead, a "bug" can be used secretly to listen to a room 24 hours a day. The bug can be connected to the listening post by cable, or it can transmit radio signals.

▷ The photograph shows some of the evidence collected by US intelligence agents when they arrested KGB agent Vladimir Izmaylov. It includes a miniature recorder for taping conversations and milk cartons containing money and equipment for making contacts.

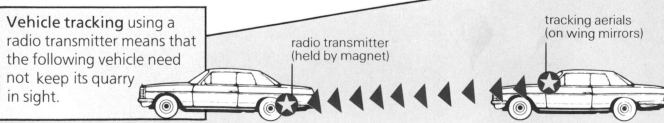

Vehicle tracking using a radio transmitter means that the following vehicle need not keep its quarry in sight.

radio transmitter (held by magnet)

tracking aerials (on wing mirrors)

In order to plant the bug, it is necessary to get inside the target room. This sometimes involves breaking and entering premises illegally but new technologies are making it easier. Sometimes the bug can be as simple as a pen or ashtray, with a microphone radio transmitter concealed inside.

A modern and sophisticated method of bugging is to listen not to conversation, but to sound or electronic emissions from typewriters or computers. This sound can be analyzed in order to find out what was typed. Some embassies in London and Washington have been bugged like this. Then the British or American secret services can read an ambassador's letters to his government before they have even been sent out of the embassy.

▽ The new Soviet embassy in Washington DC showing how the US agents could bug the building. The Soviet Union and the United States have agreed to build each other new embassy buildings. This has been the subject of much controversy as each side has accused the other of inserting tiny electronic circuits into the concrete structure of the new buildings.

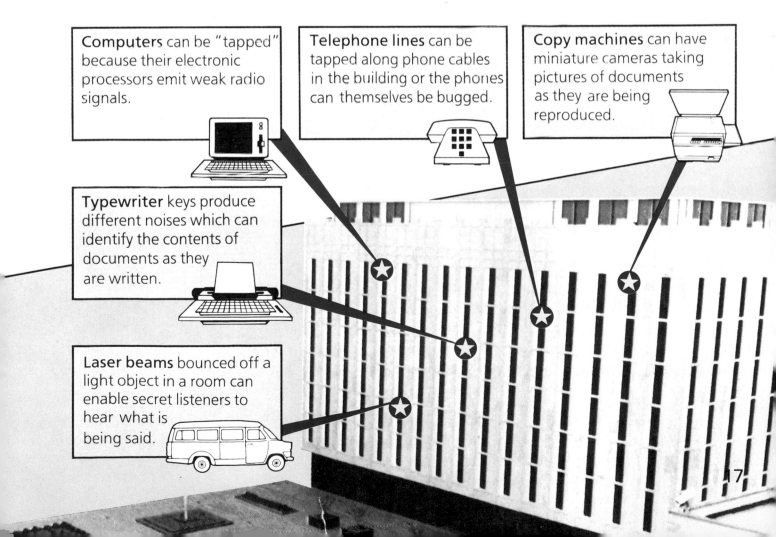

Computers can be "tapped" because their electronic processors emit weak radio signals.

Telephone lines can be tapped along phone cables in the building or the phones can themselves be bugged.

Copy machines can have miniature cameras taking pictures of documents as they are being reproduced.

Typewriter keys produce different noises which can identify the contents of documents as they are written.

Laser beams bounced off a light object in a room can enable secret listeners to hear what is being said.

Spy satellites

Only the United States and the Soviet Union can afford the most sophisticated and expensive type of spy equipment — spy satellites. Satellites, such as the American "Keyhole," (KH-11), can take very detailed pictures from over a hundred miles away in space. Soviet Cosmos and American Keyhole satellites have repeatedly photographed much of the world for almost 25 years.

◁ The giant Titan rocket is used to launch new US intelligence satellites into orbit above the earth. In 1986 Titan 3 exploded carrying a "Big Bird" spy satellite.

▽ A US "Keyhole" spy satellite picture taken from at least 90 miles away shows the first-ever Soviet nuclear-powered aircraft carrier being built on the Black Sea.

Nowadays, anyone can buy satellite pictures of any part of the earth, taken by civilian land resources satellites. Such pictures are not as accurate or detailed as those taken by military spacecraft, but can provide much information about agricultural resources or urban development. As well as the United States and the Soviet Union, France, Japan and China are all developing such photographic satellites. Radar satellites have also been developed and keep watch on ocean shipping.

Another type of satellite does not take pictures but listens instead for electronic signals, such as radar pulses or missile control messages. This type of satellite is called a signals intelligence or "sigint" satellite. In 1987, it was revealed that Britain planned to be the third country to launch such an electronic spy satellite. The new British satellite, called Zircon, would be listening to Soviet radio signals by the early 1990s.

Spy aircraft and ships are still used alongside the satellites. The American SR-71 is the most advanced spy plane. Ships, often disguised as merchant vessels, keep track of the movements of all classes of ships. In the early 1980s Sweden dropped depth charges when it suspected that an unidentified submarine was hiding near its shoreline.

△ The high-flying U-2 spy plane was developed in the 1950s and used for spy missions directly over Soviet territory. In a famous incident, the Soviet Union shot down an American U-2 flying over its territory in 1960 and captured the pilot, Gary Powers. He was exchanged in 1962 for a Soviet master spy.

▽ Satellite tracking dishes at the US National Security Agency station at Menwith Hill, in northern England, are linked to the newest US spy satellites. These satellites "hover" in a position 24,000 miles away from earth, listening to radio signals.

Human agents

Secret agents are still used to gather information. Recruiting and running secret agents is a difficult and dangerous business for both the spy and his or her contact.

Some agents meet their contacts face to face to pass on information. A more common method is the "dead letter drop." The agent and contact arrange to leave information for each other in a public place. They deposit and collect this information at different times so they cannot be seen together.

A double agent is a spy who works for one secret service and has been detected by or approaches another hostile secret service in order to spy for them instead. Controlling a double agent is especially difficult for secret services – how can they know which side the agent really works for? Defectors, agents who leave one country for another, are often suspected of being double agents.

△ This photograph was taken in July 1966 and shows KGB agent Valentin Revin checking a specified telephone directory for tiny marks which will contain a coded message for him. Spy "tradecraft" consists of the secret methods an agent uses to make contact with her or his handler, and to send information. Secret codes, radio transmitters and invisible inks are all still popular methods.

△ In May 1985 John Walker was arrested for spying. Further investigation revealed that he had been selling the Soviets secrets for 17 years. As an officer on board a US nuclear submarine, he had had access to much useful information.

△ Walker's brother Arthur was also arrested, as was John's son Michael. Arthur had been an anti-submarine warfare specialist. Michael was a sailor on the aircraft carrier *Nimitz*. They gave John documents which he passed to his Soviet contact.

△ Anthony Blunt was discovered by MI5 to have been a Soviet spy in 1964, when he confessed to being the "fourth" man in a spy ring. The British decided to do a deal with him and keep his treachery secret if he co-operated.

△ Nicholas Daniloff, an American journalist, was arrested in Moscow by the Soviets on suspicion of spying in September 1986. The Americans claimed he had been framed and swiftly arranged his release. Journalists are often used as agents by secret services.

△ Arkadi Shevchenko was a close adviser of the Soviet Foreign Minister, Andrei Gromyko. He was posted to the United Nations in New York and gave the Americans much useful information about Soviet intentions. Eventually he defected in April 1978.

△ Vitaly Yurchenko went missing in August 1985. In November he appeared in the Soviet embassy in Washington, claiming he had been kidnapped by US intelligence agents. The Americans said he had defected. A few days later he flew back to Moscow.

The biggest secrets

Governments often acknowledge that they operate secret services. But they usually pretend that their secret agents operate only against known hostile countries – such as NATO against the Warsaw Pact (eastern Europe). Often, however, friendly countries are at least as important a target – and agreements not to spy on your friends are broken.

In the 1960s and 1970s, British intelligence worked very hard to break the secret codes of their NATO allies, Germany and France, in order to get into the European Common Market on the best possible terms. In the 1980s France spied on Germany's Green Party because of fears that their ideas might spread to France and lead to opposition to its nuclear weapons testing program in the Pacific.

▽ In March 1987 Jonathan Pollard, who worked for US naval intelligence, pleaded guilty to spying for the Israelis. As a pro-Israeli Jew, he was eager to give secrets to Israel. He is supposed to have received nearly $45,000. The Israeli government claimed that this operation was carried out by a rogue group in its secret service, Mossad. Israel claims to prohibit its agents from spying on the United States. The affair seriously damaged US-Israeli relations.

Even more secret than foreign espionage are the operations conducted against political adversaries of the government at home. This has occurred even in liberal democratic countries, such as Canada, the United States and Australia, where people are entitled to oppose their government. Official inquiries held in the last 15 years found that security services had broken the law in order to attack political opponents.

In the United States, the Watergate affair of 1972-74 led to some major reforms. It was revealed that President Richard Nixon had known about attempts to bug the Watergate apartments and spy on his opponents. Nixon had to resign. The next presidents, Ford and Carter, then tried to control the secret agencies by allowing access to some secret documents.

Campaign for Nuclear Disarmament is a group which campaigns against nuclear arms. The telephone lines of CND members have been intercepted by British secret services.

▽ Dr. Benjamin Spock, the childcare expert, is also a leading peace campaigner. In the 1970s, British security agencies tried to intercept Spock's correspondence on behalf of US intelligence.

Disinformation

One way that secret services can be used to help one country gain political advantage over another is by spreading propaganda or "disinformation." Disinformation is another way of saying "lying by governments." Sometimes untruthful stories are planted in newspapers and magazines or on radio and television by journalists who are themselves working for a secret service.

Such stories are written by their colleagues in agencies such as the CIA, KGB or MI6, but the journalist then pretends that they are truthful news. In the 1970s CIA agents planted a story about 42 Soviets being captured by pro-Western forces in Angola. The Soviets were accused of sending military advisers to Angola. This was not true but it helped foster anti-Soviet feeling in the United States.

▽ Radio Free Europe broadcasts news and programs daily to Eastern Europe from West Germany. It has been funded indirectly by the CIA. Its purpose is to give the people in communist countries information they cannot get from their own radio stations. It also broadcasts disinformation. Eastern European governments see these as propaganda broadcasts and have set up their own radio stations broadcasting news for the people of Western Europe.

▽ Former British intelligence officer Cathy Massiter resigned from MI5 after she was asked to compile reports on CND for the government to use for political purposes.

△ Andrey Sakharov returns to Moscow in December 1986. A leading human rights activist, he was harassed by the KGB in the 1980s. When Sakharov went on hunger strike, the KGB released secret films suggesting he was remaining healthy.

Disinformation and propaganda can be divided into black, gray and white categories. White propaganda consists of true information which gives a misleading impression. Black propaganda is information which is completely untrue, or information which appears to come from a different source than its true source. Gray propaganda is a mixture of the two.

As part of its disinformation work, the Soviet KGB often circulates copies of forged US government documents to journalists in the West. In the West, the CIA coordinates a deliberate disinformation program which is designed to mislead other countries about the effectiveness of its "Star Wars" missile defense system. The British and American secret services have both secretly run black propaganda radio stations in Europe and the Middle East.

▽ Forged US, NATO and Soviet documents are often produced by rival agencies as part of a propaganda war. Often the forged documents are closely based on real documents acquired by spies and fool many experts.

NATO SECRET
SUPREME HEADQUARTERS ALLIED POWERS EUROPE
GRAND QUARTIER GENERAL DES PUISSANCES ALLIEES EN EURO
BELGIUM

FORGERY

His Excellency Joseph N.A.U. Luns   26 June 1979
The Secretary General
North Atlantic Treaty Organization
Brussels/Zaventem Autoroute
B-1110 Brussels, Belgium

Dear Joseph,

Thank you for your letter of June 25 setting out certain results of our joint work which have had, I believe, a direct and lasting effect on the formulation and realization of the allied defense program. For my part, I highly appreciate your cooperation and hope that you are equally satisfied.

On leaving the post of Supreme Allied Commander in Europe, I feel it is my duty to stress once again certain aspects of allied strategy which demand our further attention and effort.

As you know, one of our presuppositions in nuclear planning is that under certain circumstances likely to develop in Europe, we may be forced to make first use of nuclear weapons. This obviously requires that allied nuclear deterrent should be strengthened and that U.S. strategic systems tightened...

◁ Clive Ponting, a senior official of the British Ministry of Defense, decided to risk his job and reveal that the government was deliberately misleading parliament about the Falklands War. So he sent copies of official documents to a member of parliament.

he shall be guilty of felony, and shall be liable to penal ser for any term not less than three years and not exceeding

Freedom of information

In democratic countries, government secrecy is a special problem for those elected to congress or parliament. How can they truly represent the people who have elected them if they and their electors are not entitled to know what the government is doing?

Freedom of information laws have now been passed in many countries, notably the United States, Sweden, Australia, and other European and English-speaking countries. These laws give any citizen the right to see most government information, except in special areas such as military secrets. Usually, people can also ask for and get details of any government files about them personally. They can then check that the government's files do not include inaccurate information, or information which should not be kept about their lives.

In Britain, the government does not want to have freedom of information laws. It believes that people should accept that what the government does is always right, without wanting to check the information on which government decisions are based. But members of parliament (MPs) and organizations who want freedom of information laws say that the government will be able to make better decisions if information about the decision is openly discussed first.

◁ The Argentinian battleship, *General Belgrano*, was sunk at the start of the Falklands War, with the loss of 368 lives. Ponting claimed that the British government had concealed the real reasons they sank the *Belgrano*. The documents he leaked helped to show exactly what the British government knew when the decision to sink was taken. Clive Ponting was prosecuted under the notorious catch-all Section 2 of the British Official Secrets Acts – but he was found not guilty by the trial jury.

The right to know

Even the ancient Romans and Greeks were perplexed about the problem of who watches the watchers. Do you create a special organization in order to check what the secret service is doing and how efficient it is? In some countries, government officials think that neither the public nor members of parliament or congress should know anything about intelligence gathering. They say national security must come first and secret services must remain secret.

But if a secret service is not carefully supervised by the government, many things can go wrong. It may become corrupt or inefficient, or start pursuing the wrong targets. Money may be wasted or laws broken. Because of many experiences of this kind, most Western governments have appointed small groups of members of parliament, or judges, or others to exercise supervision over secret service work. For example, permission is usually required from a judge or an outside body before a secret service is allowed to tap a telephone line or to break into someone's house to plant a bug or copy private papers.

▽ In October 1987 the Soviets showed a group of foreign journalists and specialists around its chemical weapons factory in Shikhany, 375 miles from Moscow. In November the Americans showed the Soviets around their factories. This is part of a new policy of greater openness or *glasnost* by the Soviet Union. In order to achieve reduction in nuclear weapons, both the Soviet Union and the United States have to be able to show publicly that they are undertaking their part of the deal and allow the other side's observers to verify their actions. Less secrecy is now on the agenda.

Intelligence operations are important when critical international events could start a war. During the Persian Gulf confrontations between Irani and Iraqi forces and other countries' tankers, both US and Soviet intelligence resources were fully deployed to protect their and their allies' shipping from attack.

Outside supervision of secret service work by members of parliament is said to make the intelligence services accountable to parliament and thus to the people who elected it. People who are in favor of more accountability for secret services believe that although some secrets may be given away, the result will still be better protection for the national security of the country concerned.

Spy facts

Types of intelligence

SIGINT: Signals intelligence is information gathered from the unauthorized reception and analysis of foreign communications messages. Sigint includes breaking codes which are often used by governments to conceal the contents of a message being transmitted.

HUMINT: Human intelligence is information gathered by people, including secret agents and informers.

ELINT: Electronic intelligence is information gathered by monitoring the electronic signals of a foreign country or military force.

PHOTINT: Photographic intelligence is information obtained from pictures taken by spy satellites, or by high altitude spy planes such as the U-2 or SR-71.

Major intelligence agencies

United States
CIA   Central Intelligence Agency
FBI   Federal Bureau of Investigation
NSA   National Security Agency
DIA   Defense Intelligence Agency

Soviet Union
KGB   Committee for State Security
GRU   Chief (Military) Intelligence Directorate

United Kingdom
SIS   Secret Intelligence Service (MI6)
SS   Security Service (MI5)
GCHQ   Government Communications Headquarters
DIS   Defense Intelligence Staff

France
DGSE   Foreign Espionage Directorate
DST   National Surveillance Directorate (Security Service)
GCR   Radio and Electronic Surveillance Agency

West Germany
BfV   Office for the Protection of the Constitution
BND   Federal Intelligence Service
ASBW   Military Security Service

East Germany
MfS   Ministry for State Security
HVA   Chief Intelligence Directorate

Israel
Mossad   Foreign Intelligence Service
Shin Beth   Security Service

South Africa
NIS   National Intelligence Service

Australia
ASIO   Australian Security Intelligence Organization
ASIS   Australian Secret Intelligence Service
DSD   Defense Signals Division

Canada
SIS   Security Intelligence Service
CSE   Communications Security Establishment

China
CELD   Central External Liaison Department

◁ The KGB symbol.

Chronology

1963 Kim Philby, a British journalist, defects to the Soviet Union. He is the "third man" in a British spy ring.

1964 Anthony Blunt confesses to being the "fourth man" in the British spy ring. Not revealed publicly until 1979.

1973 Roger Hollis, former head of MI5, dies. Some British intelligence experts think he was the "fifth man" in the British spy ring.

1975 US investigations reveal that the CIA was behind three assassinations: Patrice Lumumba in Congo (Zaire), Rafael Trujillo in Dominican Republic and Ngo Dinh Diem in Vietnam.

1977 Admiral Stansfield Turner becomes director of the CIA and cuts large numbers of staff in an attempt to bring the CIA under control.

1978 Arkadi Shevchenko defects to the United States and starts a new career advising US intelligence agencies.

1979 Stanislas Levchenko defects to the United States revealing details of Soviet disinformation in the West.

1980 CIA massively expands under President Reagan.

1983 Geoffrey Prime, a former employee of Britain's GCHQ, is found guilty of spying for the Soviets.

1985 Members of the Walker family in the United States are exposed as spies.

1985 French agents blow up the *Rainbow Warrior* in New Zealand.

1985 Vitaly Yurchenko "defects" to the United States and then returns to Moscow.

1986 The United States and the Soviet Union exchange KGB officer Gennadi Zakharov for American journalist Nicholas Daniloff.

1986 Colonel Oliver North is fired when it is discovered that money from a secret arms-for-hostages deal with Iran was sent to fund the Nicaraguan *Contras*.

1987 Jonathan Pollard is found guilty of spying on the United States for Israel.

1987 A Congress investigation of the Iran-*Contra* scandal blames President Reagan for not keeping control of covert operations.

Index

Photographic Credits:
Cover and pages 11 (right), 20 and 21 (top left, top centre and bottom left): Associated Press; pages 4-5, 8 (top), 12, 13, (top), 14 (left and right), 16, 23, 24, 25 and 29: Rex Features; pages 6, 17, 18-19, 25 and 30: Duncan Campbell; pages 7, 10 (left), 13 (bottom), 15, 18, 19, 26, 28 and back cover: Frank Spooner Agency; pages 8 (bottom), 10 (right – both), 21 (top right, bottom centre and bottom right) and 22: Popperfoto; pages 11 (left) and 24: Stern; page 26 (inset): Financial Times.

PRINTED IN BELGIUM BY
proost
INTERNATIONAL BOOK PRODUCTION